Gifts To Make

This edition first published 1988 by
The Hamlyn Publishing Group Limited
Michelin House
81 Fulham Road
London
SW3 6RB
England
By arrangement with Ellsyd Press
an imprint of David Ell Press Pty Ltd
137-139 Regent Street, Chippendale 2008
Australia

ISBN 0 600 559 939

Printed in Hong Kong through Colorcraft Ltd

Gifts To Make

ANNE INGRAM

PEGGY O'DONNELL

Illustrations by
MARK DAVID

HAMLYN

For
THE L.C.Ls.
with love

Contents

Let's do it together

This book is jam-packed full of ideas. Ideas that can be turned into presents for the family or your friends. It is also a fun book, full of things to make – from loo-paper holders to jigsaw puzzles, from cheese in a pot to painted hats.

Planning and making a present is as much fun as giving or receiving one, especially when you share the making with someone else. In fact, all the things in this book should be made by two people, doing it together, sharing the fun.

Once you have decided that you will make a special present for Aunt Anne's birthday, or Grandma Peg's retirement, or Cousin Bob's Christmas, then plan it carefully, don't rush. It's no good starting the day before (unless it's a cooking present you have decided on) because a rushed job usually looks just that – rushed.

Before you begin, read the instructions, make sure you have *all* the materials required, then decide where you will need to work, checking first that it's OK to use that spot – and leave it tidy.

Take care when using other people's tools, kitchen utensils, sewing machine or whatever and always leave them clean and return them to their proper place. Handle knives, scissors and saws with care and don't play silly games with them because that's when accidents happen.

Handy hints

Read these next few pages because these handy hints really do help!

Odds-and-ends box

Every family needs one. It's a box into which everyone throws all those odd things – like shells, buttons, old birthday cards, scraps of material, screws, anything that you know will come in handy one day for something. This box can be a real treasure trove when it comes to making gifts.

Cutting cardboard

Always cut *into* the corners when you are cutting out an awkward shape. When cutting out a circle, make a hole in the middle with the point of the scissors first, then begin your cut around the edge.

Gluing paper or cardboard

Place plenty of sheets of newspaper, fully opened, on the work bench, then you can change the top sheet each time you glue something.

Spread a thin layer of glue onto both surfaces, remember a little will stick as well as a lot if you have spread it evenly and taken it right to the edges.

Always allow the glue a few minutes to become tacky before joining the two pieces.

Removing labels

When you need to remove labels from glass, plastic or cans, soak them in warm water. To remove the glue left by the labels, a little methylated spirit on a cloth will do the job.

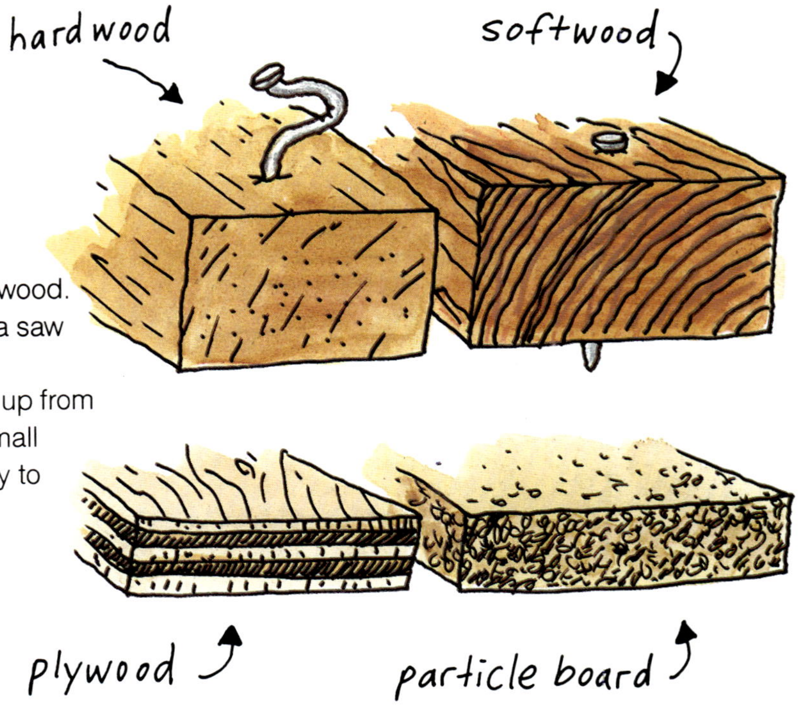

Choosing wood

Choose softwood in preference to hardwood. Hardwoods are heavy, hard to cut with a saw and the nails are inclined to bend.

Plywoods and chipboard are made up from thin layers of wood glued together or small chips of wood. They are not always easy to work with and will swell when wet.

Know your tools

Hammer – always work on a flat surface holding your wood firmly (with two of you working together, this is much easier). Hold the hammer near the end of the handle, not close to the head. Face the hammer head straight down onto the top of the nail so that you hit it in the centre. If you hit the nail on the side it will bend (if this happens pull it out and start again).

Saw – two of you are needed when sawing because it's hard work. If one of you holds the end that is being sawn off, the one using the saw can rest their knee on the other end, and the wood will stay steady.

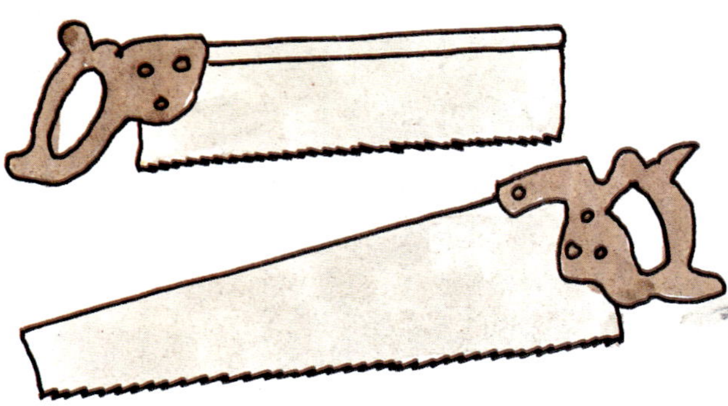

Hand drill and bit – choose the size of the bit to fit the screws you are going to use. Always keep your hand drill straight while drilling. If you drill a hole and use screws you will make a stronger join than just nailing, which can often split the wood.

Screws and screwdriver – choose the screwdriver that fits the top of the screw. Choose the screw that suits what you are doing, but a flat-headed wood screw is what you'll need for the ideas in this book.

Knots you will need

We have suggested you use the following knots in this book, so here's how to tie them:

A reef knot:

Figure eight knot:

Round turn and two half hitches:

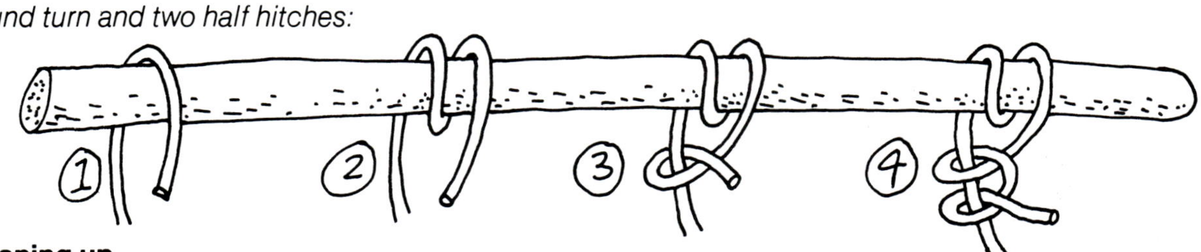

Cleaning up

It's a good idea to put things away as you finish with them, then you don't have a great pile of mess to tidy up at the end. Leave the kitchen tidy and wash up all the things you have used. Return all tools to the tool box. Put the sewing machine away.

If you have used paints, wash out the brushes as soon as you have used them, otherwise they will go hard.

Scary things

These make great gifts for all your friends (they are not so good for adults!).

Egg box spiders

You will need:

1 egg box
1 sheet of lightweight cardboard
contact glue
poster paints
shirring or hat elastic
bodkin
2 sequins or buttons

How to make:

Cut two cups from the egg box. Through one cup thread a knotted length of elastic (figure eight knot) so that the knot is caught inside the cup. Into the bottom of the second cup glue a tightly rolled up ball of newspaper (this is to add weight).

Glue the two cups together and paint all over – choose a nice scary colour! While the paint is drying measure, cut and fold the cardboard legs (as shown), remembering you need 8 legs for a spider.

Paint the legs a different scary colour to the body, then glue them to the body (as shown). Glue the sequins or buttons on for the eyes and paint on a white mouth.

Make at least 6 spiders to give to the one friend, all in different colours.

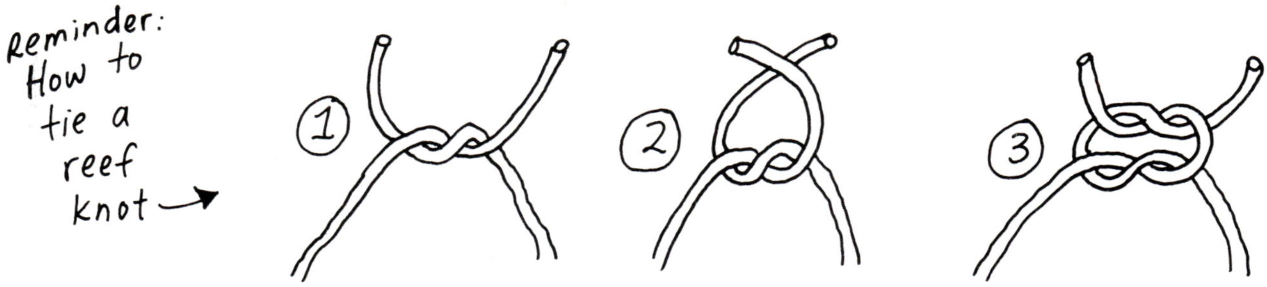

Monster mask

You will need:

1 paper plate 25 cm across
1 egg box
contact glue
shirring or hat elastic
bodkin
poster paints
sequins, buttons or dried peas
a sheet of newspaper

How to make:

Using the bodkin, thread the elastic through two sides of the plate and tie with a reef knot. Make sure the holes are opposite each other so that the mask sits straight on your face. Tighten the elastic to the size of your head.

Put the mask on and measure where your eyes will come. Mark with a pencil, then cut two small holes. Next, cut two cups from the egg box, removing the tops from these to make a hole, then glue the cups over your eye holes.

Cut another egg box cup and glue this on for a nose. Now you have to paint your monster face all over, so plan your colours carefully because you need to paint on a scary mouth, with horrible teeth, and these need to show up against the background colour.

When the paint is dry, glue on the sequins (or buttons or dried peas) as horrible bumps on the cheeks.

To make the hair and the beard, begin by painting both sides of the sheet of newspaper (choose a mad colour like purple or orange). Be careful when painting the newspaper – do one side and allow it to dry thoroughly before doing the other.

When dry, cut long and short strips off the newspaper. Glue the long ones on as hair, which can fall all over your face and down your back. The short ones make a great beard.

Toffee fun

A sticky treat for everyone!

Simple toffee

You will need:

2 cups of sugar

½ cup of water

½ level teaspoon cream of tartar

1 teaspoon vinegar

How to make:

Grease a shallow baking tin, put to one side.

Place all ingredients in saucepan. Stir over moderate heat until sugar is dissolved and the mixture boils. Boil gently until the syrup becomes honey- coloured, then remove from heat immediately. Pour into baking tin and mark into squares as it cools.

These variations are worth trying:

- a topping of crushed nuts, coconut, hundreds and thousands or sultanas may be sprinkled on the toffee before it sets
- set the toffee in paper patty-cake cases
- add a cup of shelled peanuts as the toffee is removed from the heat.

Toffee apples

You will need:

hot toffee as in previous recipe
5 apples
5 wooden skewers
few drops of cochineal

How to make:

Wash and dry the apples, insert skewers.

Make the simple toffee recipe, add a few drops of cochineal to the hot toffee. Dip apples, one at a time, tilting the saucepan to give greater depth.

Place coated apples on a greased tray to set.

You can make your apples any colour by using different food colourings.

For bird lovers

Bird feeding tray

The ideal gift for bird lovers who want to encourage the seed-eaters to their garden. It can be hung from the branch of a tree, or from a balcony.

You will need:

1 old tin or plastic baking dish, tray or plate
4 pieces of strong, thick string of equal length

How to make:

If using an old tin baking dish, tray or plate, you will make the four holes with a hammer and a fat nail.

If using an old plastic tray or plate, you will make the four holes with a hand drill and a bit.

Make sure the holes are big enough for the string to fit through. Fasten the string underneath by using a figure eight knot to prevent it slipping through.

Pine cone bird feeder

This is an ideal feeder for smaller birds, or for a small garden. You will need to find an open pine cone for this feeder to be successful. If you can only find closed ones, then ask an adult to place it in a warm oven until it opens.

You will need:

1 open pine cone
1 jar of peanut butter
1 packet birdseed
1 piece of soft wire

How to make:

Around the top of the open pine cone attach the soft wire.

Roll small balls of peanut butter in birdseed, then push into open sections of the pine cone (as shown).

Bird pudding

This is a feeder for larger, meat-eating birds.

You will need:

equal parts of the following:

- dripping
- honey
- dried pea flour (pease-meal)
- instant porridge

4 large buttons

4 pieces of string about 1 metre long

How to make:

Melt the dripping in a saucepan. Stir in the honey. When mixed, beat in the pea flour and porridge until the mixture turns into a thick paste.

Thread a piece of string through a button, then mould the mixture around it. Make up four puddings (they keep well in the fridge).

Hang one in a tree – well out of the reach of cats.

Stilts for fun and games

There are two types of stilts to choose from. One is made of old tins and string and is quick and easy to put together – and ideal for younger friends. The other is made from wood and will take time and patience (and help) – and is great for older friends.

Can stilts

You will need:
2 large drink cans
2 pieces of strong string
acrylic paint
hammer and nail

How to make:
Choose two cans the same height and width. They need to be big enough for your feet to fit comfortably.

Thoroughly wash the cans, removing the labels, then paint them with a fancy design. When the paint is dry, make two holes opposite each other near the closed end of the cans. Use a hammer and a nail to make the holes.

Thread the string through the holes. Take the string to about the height of the friend you are giving them to and join the two ends with a reef knot. The strings can be adjusted to suit each user by moving the reef knot.

Wooden stilts

You will need:
2 long pieces of wood
2 blocks of wood
4 coach bolts
4 wing nuts
hand drill and bit

How to make:
Visit a timber yard and choose the two long pieces of wood carefully. They need to be thin enough for you to grip, yet strong enough to hold your weight and long enough to extend about 50 cm above your head when you're standing on the ground.

While at the timber yard hunt round for two off-cuts – these blocks make the ideal foot rests for your stilts. Try and get more than two because they may split.

Bolt the foot rests to the handles and tighten the wing nuts. Your stilts are ready to go – but it takes practice.

The coach bolts need to be long enough to go right through both pieces of timber – that is the stilt handle and the foot rest, so buy the bolts and wing nuts *after* you have purchased the wood (as shown).

Find a bit that's the right size for the bolts, then drill 2 holes through each foot rest block (as shown).

Measure up the handles so that the bottom of the foot rest blocks will be 20 cm from the ground.

Hold each block in position and, with a pencil, make a mark through the holes. With two of you doing this you'll get it right first go. Now drill your holes through the handles.

Cocoa capers

For the chocolate lover.

Chocolate fudge

You will need:

2½ cups of caster sugar

1 level teaspoon of cream of tartar

3 level tablespoons of cocoa or drinking chocolate

1 cup milk

1½ tablespoons of margarine (or butter)

How to make:

Grease a shallow cake tin and put to one side. Into a saucepan put sugar, cocoa and cream of tartar; mix in milk. Stir over heat until the sugar is dissolved and the mixture boils. Keep boiling as quickly as possible till the mixture forms a soft ball when a spoonful is dropped in cold water.

Remove from heat and beat in margarine. Continue beating until the mixture thickens and the margarine is absorbed. Pour into prepared tin. Mark into squares as it cools.

Chocolate biscuits

You will need:

½ cup of margarine (or butter)
1 cup of sugar
2 cups of self-raising flour
1 egg
2 tablespoons of cocoa

How to make:

Melt margarine, then mix sugar into margarine. Cool. Add flour, cocoa and egg. Mix well. Roll into log shape and slice into rounds approximately 5 cm thick. Bake in a moderately hot oven for 10 minutes.

Chocolate cake

You will need:

1 heaped tablespoon of cocoa
2 tablespoons of hot water
¾ cup of margarine (or butter)
¾ cup of sugar
2 eggs
vanilla essence
1 cup of self-raising flour

How to make:

In a small basin mix the cocoa with hot water and stir until smooth. In a separate bowl, cream margarine and sugar, then add the cocoa mixture. Lightly mix the eggs and vanilla, and beat into the creamed mixture. Loosely fold in the flour. Cook in 2 well-greased shallow cake tins in a moderate oven for 25 minutes. Cool. Fill the centre and spread the top with chocolate icing. Decorate with chopped nuts, coconut or sultanas.

Chocolate icing:

Mix 2 cups of icing sugar, 1 tablespoon of cocoa and 2 tablespoons of water to a smooth paste.

Gifts for grandma

Gran will always love anything you make specially for her, so try these two ideas.

A self-portrait

You will need:

1 large sheet of lining paper
scissors
poster paints or felt-tip pens
marker pen

How to make:

Spread the lining paper out on a smooth, hard floor, making sure there are no wrinkles in the paper.

Lie flat on the paper, keeping your hands flat and your fingers wide apart. Now ask your helper to draw carefully around you with the marker pen.

When the outline is finished, place the paper on your workbench; now you can take over and paint your own portrait.

Using poster paints or felt-tip pens, paint in your face, then your clothes. Try and make it look as much like you as possible. When dry, cut yourself out following the line of the marker pen.

Jewelled brooch

You will need:

1 sheet of thick cardboard
contact glue
a selection of buttons, shells, beads, sequins, macaroni, dried peas
1 large safety pin
sticking plaster

How to make:

First plan the shape and size of the brooch you are going to make by sketching it out on some scrap paper. It could be an oval shape, or square, or a star, it could even be Gran's initial, but decide all this *before* you start drawing on your piece of cardboard.

Having decided the shape and the size, measure and draw the outline – in pencil – on the cardboard, then cut out your design. Cover the top surface with glue and arrange the buttons, shells, dried peas or whatever, on the glue in an attractive design.

Leave to dry thoroughly, then turn it over and attach the safety pin with pieces of sticking plaster. Make sure the pin is in the right place so that the brooch balances correctly and doesn't tip to one side all the time.

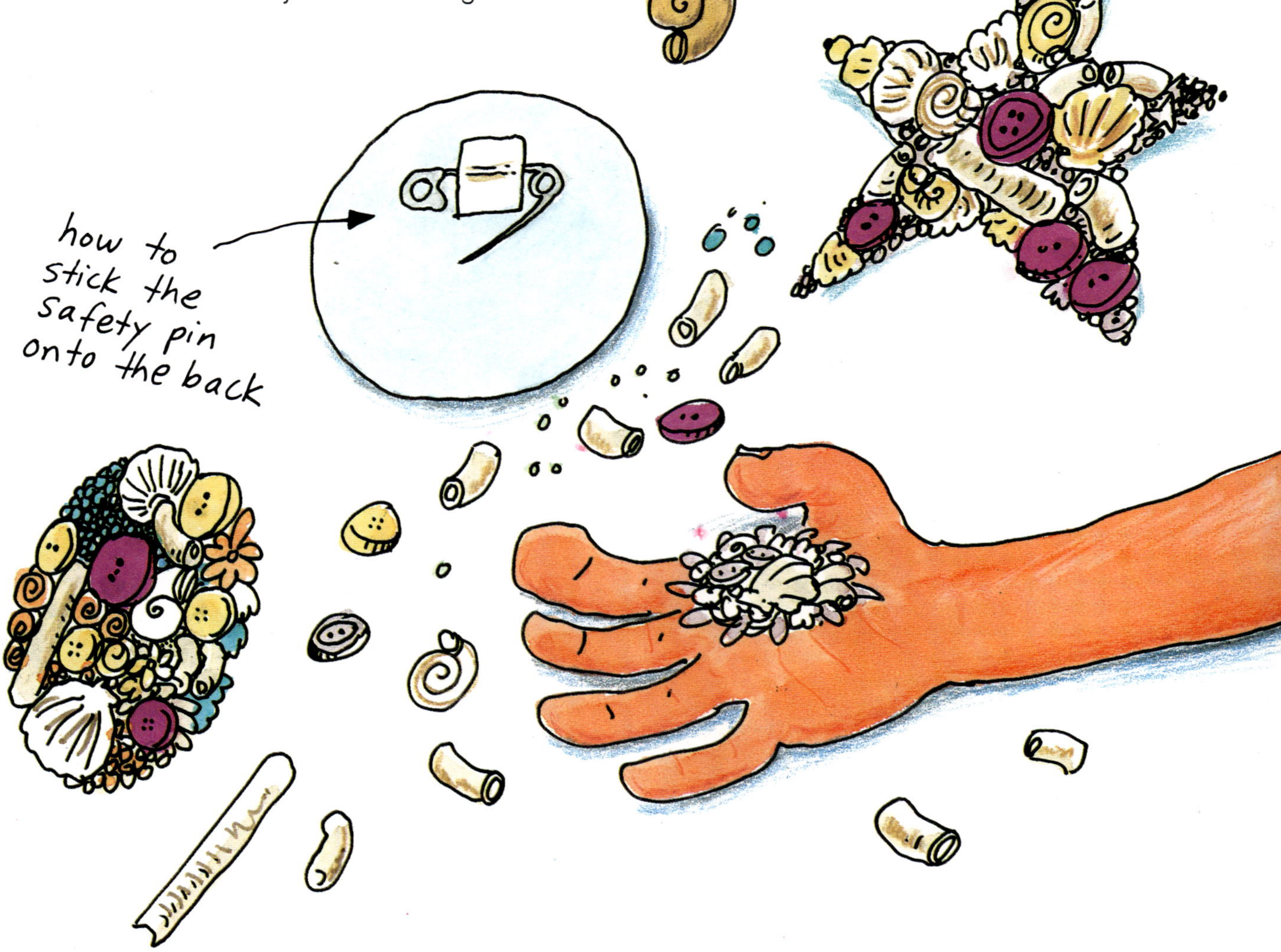

Bright clothes

Nowadays, with fabric paints and cold water dyes readily available in art and craft shops, it is possible to design very personal gifts for your family or friends.

In fact the choice of things to decorate is amazing:

- hats
- sneekers
- scarves
- handkerchiefs
- pillowcases
- towels
- T-shirts
- shorts
- socks
- gardening gloves

anything at all, so long as it's *NOT* acrylic or terylene (check on the instruction sheets provided with the dyes).

Before you begin, decide whether you want a basic colour for the article, or whether you will use fabric paints only. For example, you could decide to give Aunt Anne a green scarf with a dragon design. You would use a cold water green dye first, before you begin painting your fabulous dragon with the fabric paints.

You will need:
a selection of fabric paints
a selection of cold water dyes
an enamel dish
plenty of newspaper to cover where you will be working
salt and washing soda (these are to fix the dye)

How to make:
Read all the instructions before you start, talk them over together and make sure you understand what you will be doing.

Cover your work area carefully with plenty of newspaper because cold water dyes are colour fast (they won't wash out), but while they are wet they will dye everything they touch – *so be careful!* This is why we suggest you use an enamel dish for dyeing – don't use the washing machine or it will change colour!

When doing designs on fabrics it's a good idea to plan them out first on paper – you can then see how they are going to look. When designing sneekers or hats you can work straight on to them with a pencil design first.

Bits and pieces

Draught stopper

The ideal gift for people who live in a cold climate.

You will need:
5 pairs of worn-out socks
old stockings
coloured wools
darning needle

How to make:
Save all the worn-out socks and laddered stockings over a few months. If you can get bright and striped socks your draught stopper will look even better.

Stuff one toe end firmly, then sew on a sock leg with a darning needle and coloured wool. Now stuff that portion, then sew on another sock leg, then stuff it – and so on until you come to the end. Stuff the end toe *before* you sew it on.

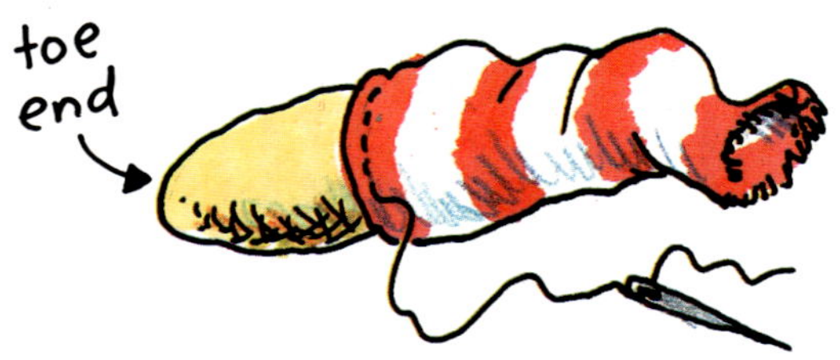

Sew on two buttons as eyes and you have a *snake draught stopper!*

Fluffy doll

Fluffy animals are always a popular gift with the very young, or as a decoration for the bed.

You will need:

a selection of wools – various colours
a sheet of cardboard
bodkin
glue
a selection of felts – various colours

How to make:

Cut two circles out of the cardboard, then cut a large hole in the centre of each (make sure they are exactly the same). The size of these circles determines the size of the pompom you will make.

To make a pompom, place the two cardboard circles together and use the bodkin to wind the wool round and round them. When you have finished, drop glue into the centre of the cardboard circles so that it holds the wool firmly (as shown).

When glue is dry, cut between the two circles of cardboard, then knot a length of wool tightly round the centre (reef knot), leaving a long thread which will help when sewing the pieces together. Remove the cardboard rings. Make the next pompom.

Attach the pompom head to the pompom body. Cut the shapes for the eyes, nose and mouth out of the felt and glue to the face.

The hair is made by plaiting the wool and gluing it on. The arms and legs can either be plaits or small pompoms.

You can make lots of interesting gifts out of these pompoms, like fluffy snakes or fluffy cats, just let your imagination run wild.

Practical presents

Loo-paper holder

This is a very practical present. It sits in the loo and holds the spare rolls of loo-paper!

You will need:

1 piece of softwood 14 cm square and 1.5 cm thick
1 dowel stick 40 cm long
1 piece of softwood 10 cm square and 1.5 cm thick
hand drill
bit – big enough to fit dowel stick
saw
wood glue
paint
sandpaper

How to make:

In the centre of the 14 cm square softwood, drill a hole about 1 cm deep. Drill carefully, because your dowel stick must stand straight in this hole. Glue the dowel into the hole and leave to dry.

Take the 10 cm square softwood and measure 1.5 cm down on each corner, rule a line across and carefully saw off each corner (as shown). Sandpaper these corners smooth.

With the help of the person working with you, drill a hole in the centre of one side of this piece of wood (as shown) – this is for the other end of the dowel, so use the same bit as before. When placed on top of the dowel this piece of wood must sit straight, it must also lift smoothly on and off the dowel, so sandpaper if necessary.

Now paint everything in one colour. When dry, take the top off the dowel and paint on the pig's face (as shown), marking an outline with a pencil first.

The holder is now ready to store three rolls of loo-paper.

Knife holder

The ideal gift for a family with young children, it keeps the sharp knives well out of their reach.

You will need:

1 piece of softwood 30 cm x 8 cm x 1.5 cm
1 piece of softwood 30 cm x 5 cm x 0.5 cm
2 pieces of softwood 5 cm x 2 cm x 0.5 cm
4 screws 1.5 cm long
hand drill and bit
paint
sandpaper

How to make:

Cut the softwood to size, making sure all measurements are correct. Smooth off all rough edges with sandpaper and paint all pieces to match the kitchen.

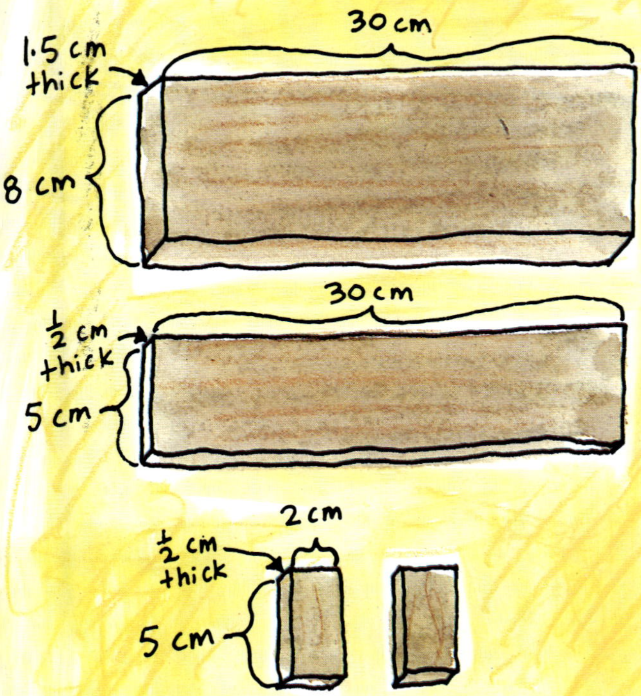

The next step will require two of you to hold and align the wood. Place the largest piece of wood flat on the work bench, then rest the two smallest pieces of wood, one on either side, aligned with the bottom, then place the last piece of wood on top of these (as shown).

Using the hand drill, fitted with a bit the size of the screws, drill two holes at each end down through the three pieces of wood (as shown). Screw together and tighten.

So that the knife holder can be attached to the kitchen wall, drill two holes in the top of the largest piece of wood (as shown). It's a nice idea to give this present with the two screws ready to attach it to the wall.

Savoury gifts

You will always have some friends who don't like sweet things, so give them something savoury to nibble.

Nuts and bolts

You will need:

1 small packet of Nutra-Grain
500 g salted peanuts
1 packet of cream of chicken soup
1 packet of French onion soup
1 dessertspoon curry powder
1 teaspoon dry mustard
½ cup oil

How to make:

Warm the oil. Mix all the dry ingredients together in a large bowl. When thoroughly mixed, pour the warm oil over them and mix.

Leave standing in bowl for one hour stirring every 10 minutes until all oil is absorbed and the whole mixture is dry.

Store in an air tight jar.

Cheese in a pot

You will need:

125 g blue vein cheese
125 g cream cheese
125 g cheddar cheese
60 g butter
1 teaspoon chives
cayene pepper (a pinch)

How to make:

Beat the blue vein cheese until smooth. Add the cream and the cheddar cheeses, plus butter, blend well. Stir in chives and cayene pepper.

Lightly grease a fancy-shaped jar or ceramic pot, spoon in mixture and keep in fridge until ready to give away.

You can vary this by using different herbs, such as basil, tarragon, parsley, marjoram, oregano or a combination of any. Another idea is crispy bacon.

For the studious

There is always someone you know who is forever sitting in front of their desk working. So help them keep it tidy – give them one of these as a gift.

Desk set

You will need:
5 large plastic drink bottles
acrylic paint – various colours
PVC tape

How to make:
Begin by soaking the labels off all the bottles and cleaning both the outside and inside thoroughly.

Next, decide what each item you are making will hold so that you know what sizes to cut. For example:

- a ruler holder will need to be about 20 cm tall
- a pencil holder will need to be about 12 cm tall
- a scissor holder about 10 cm tall
- a rubber band holder, or a paper clip holder, will only need to be 5 cm tall.

Measure and cut each plastic bottle carefully. You will need an adult to help with this because the bottles roll and are hard to cut.

Next, bind the top where you have cut with PVC tape. Then paint the outsides in designs and colours that will appeal to the person you are giving them to.

Paperweight

You will need:

1 flat-bottomed rock

acrylic paints – various colours

How to make:

First find a nice shaped rock, but make certain it has a flat bottom. Wash thoroughly, then dry. Paint to match the desk set and add it to the parcel.

Bookends

You will need:

2 house bricks

2 pieces of felt

acrylic paints – various colours

contact glue

How to make:

Try and find white house bricks, but any colour will do. Wash and dry thoroughly.

Cut the felt to the same size as the end of the brick and stick on with contact glue. Paint to match the paperweight.

Wastepaper basket

You will need:

1 large plastic ice cream container

acrylic paints – various colours

How to make:

Thoroughly wash the plastic container and remove the labels. Paint to match the rest of the set.

Paper things

Jigsaw puzzle

This is an ideal present for friends who spend a lot of time indoors.

You will need:

some old magazines
1 piece of thick cardboard
paper glue
a pair of scissors
damp sponge

How to make:

Look through the magazines (having first checked that everyone in the house has finished reading them). Choose a picture that will appeal to your friend. Carefully cut it out.

Glue the picture to the cardboard, aligning the edges of the picture with the cardboard where possible (as shown). Make certain that there are no air bumps or wrinkles (these can be carefully pushed out using a damp sponge or cloth).

Wait for the glue to dry thoroughly. With a pencil you now mark out the shape of the jigsaw, using curvy lines (as shown). Cut along these lines with the scissors. Put the jigsaw back together ready to wrap up and give away.

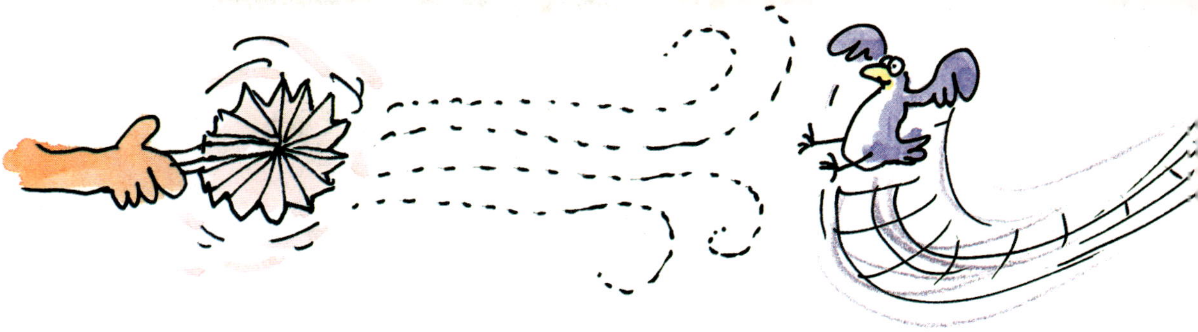

Fan for Aunty

You will need:

1 sheet of wrapping paper 15 cm x 30 cm
2 strips of cardboard 2 cm x 20 cm
paper glue

How to make:

Choose a nice bright wrapping paper, it must be a new sheet with no wrinkles in it and no fold marks. If there are, ask an adult to iron it for you using spray-on starch to remove the wrinkles.

Now fold the paper, concertina-style in 2 cm wide pleats – this needs to be done slowly and with a lot of care. Score each fold into place so that it will hold (as shown).

When the whole sheet has been pleated, fold it in half (as shown) and, using a reef knot, firmly tie the wool around this fold line. Trim away the untidy ends of wool.

Next, glue the insides together, making sure they have stuck firmly without any corners turned in. Take the two strips of cardboard and glue one to each side. Your fan is now ready to open.

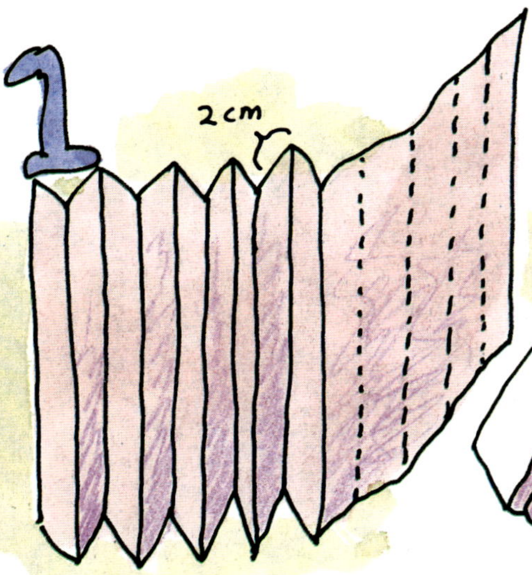

Springtime presents

For the garden lovers in your family, give them a present in the spring. You will need to plan and plant it during your summer holidays, so that it will be well established by the spring and look spectacular.

A strawberry pot

You will need:
1 large plastic bottle
potting mixture
strawberry plants
scissors
acrylic paint

How to make:
The best type of plastic bottle is the one that usually contains fruit juice. With help, cut the top section off the bottle, putting it carefully aside and retaining the lid.

Take the lower section of the bottle, wash thoroughly, removing all labels. Paint the outside in a colour, say dark green, that won't look out of place in a garden (it will certainly look better than the dirty white the plastic bottle will go).

When the paint is dry, use the scissors to push several small drainage holes in the base of the bottle. Next, carefully cut the holes around the sides of the bottle. These should be cut so that the plastic can be bent out and down to provide a small lip for the strawberry plant to rest on as it grows (as shown).

Use a potting mixture to fill the bottle, because this soil will give your young plants all they need to help them grow. Soil out of your garden could be too heavy.

Take the strawberry plants and plant them on the top of the pot and in each of the holes you have made. Water gently.

Over the next few months you must look after them, watering regularly, and once a fortnight giving them a liquid fertiliser.

A hanging pot

You will need:
the top half of the plastic bottle from the strawberry pot, with the lid
thick string
scissors
acrylic paint
curtain ring

How to make:
Take the top half of the plastic bottle and screw the lid on tightly. Wash thoroughly, removing all labels, then paint the outside.

Using the scissors, pierce one drainage hole in the lid. Then, around the top edge of your pot, pierce about 4 to 6 holes, making sure they are evenly spaced.

Measure your string into even lengths and cut the required 4 or 6 pieces. Pass one end of the string through the hole in the pot and secure it back on itself with a reef knot (as shown). Fasten all pieces in the same way. Attach the top ends of the string to the curtain ring with a reef knot.

Fill with potting soil and plant a trailing plant, such as ivy, a spider plant or petunias.

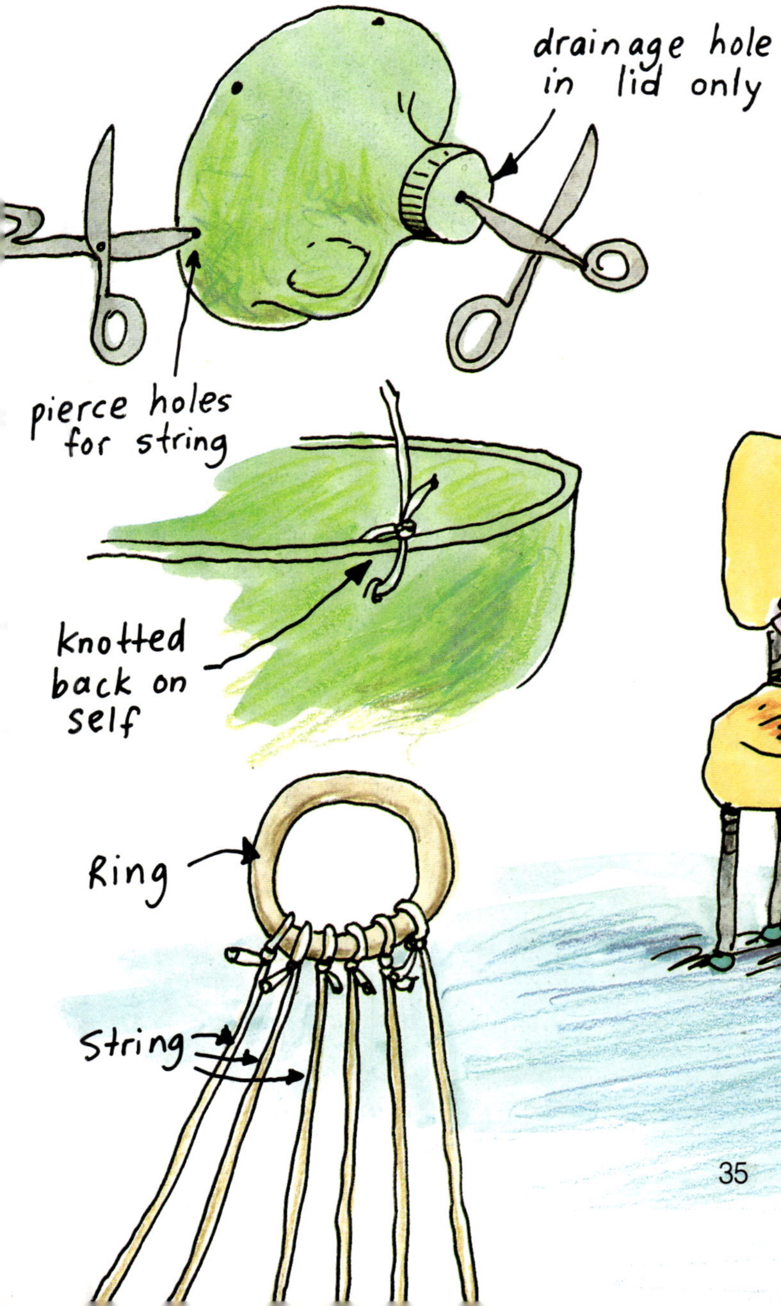

Stitch a seam

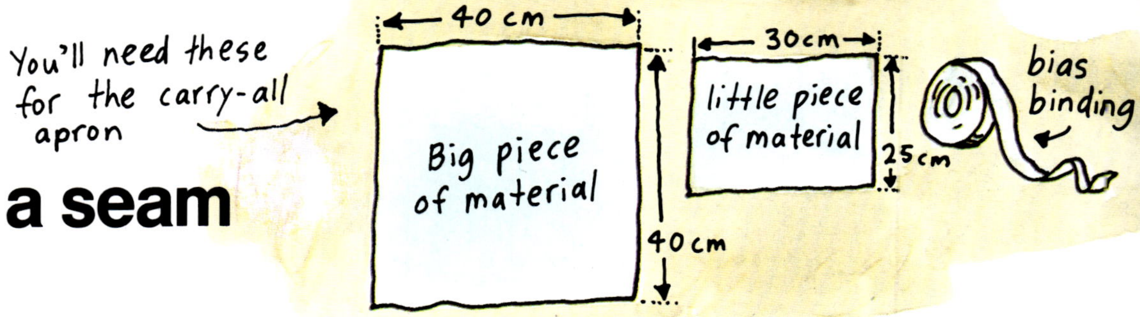

Carry-all apron

This apron is not just for using in the kitchen. With all its pockets it is ideal for wearing when gardening, cleaning-up or in the workshop.

You will need:

1 piece of plain, strong material 40 cm square

a second piece of the same material 30 cm x 25 cm

400 cm of bias binding

How to make:

Using the sewing machine, bind the four sides of the smaller piece of material with bias binding. When finished put it aside while you bind *three* sides of the other piece of material.

In the middle of the unbound edge, pin the middle of the remaining bias binding (this is to be the apron-strings), then sew on firmly (as shown).

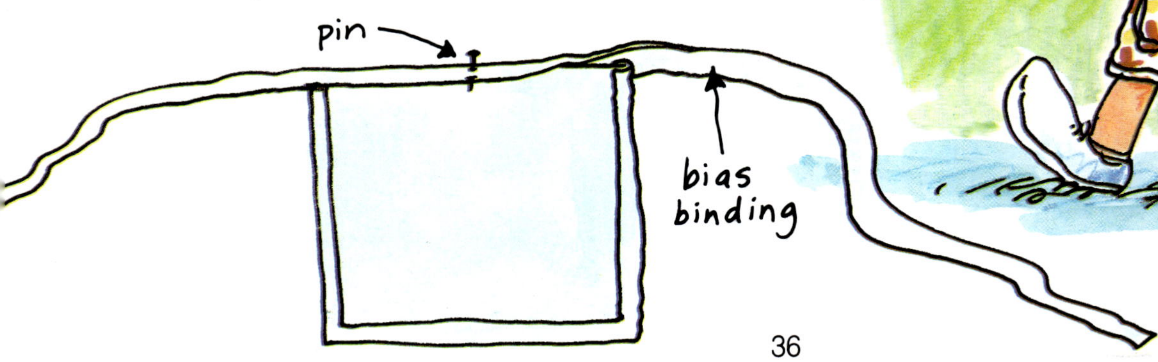

Take the smaller piece and attach it to the front of the apron, carefully sewing round three sides, then sewing several divisions down the pocket (as shown) making various smaller pockets.

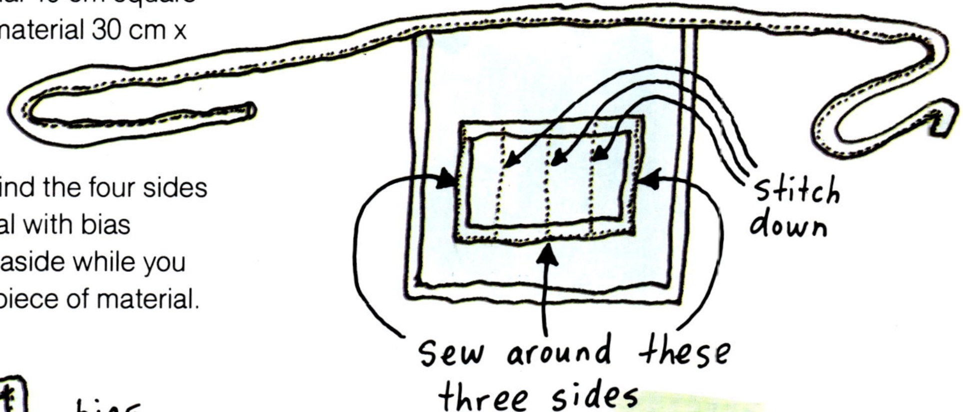

Using fabric paints and cold water dyes, decorate the apron to suit the person you are giving it to. (See BRIGHT CLOTHES on page 22).

Peg bag

This is a very practical present for the person who always has to hang out the washing.

You will need:

2 pieces of plain, strong material 30 cm square

140 cm of bias binding

Sew both pieces together on the three unbound sides then turn inside out. The bound edges are the top of the peg bag.

Decorate with fabric paints.

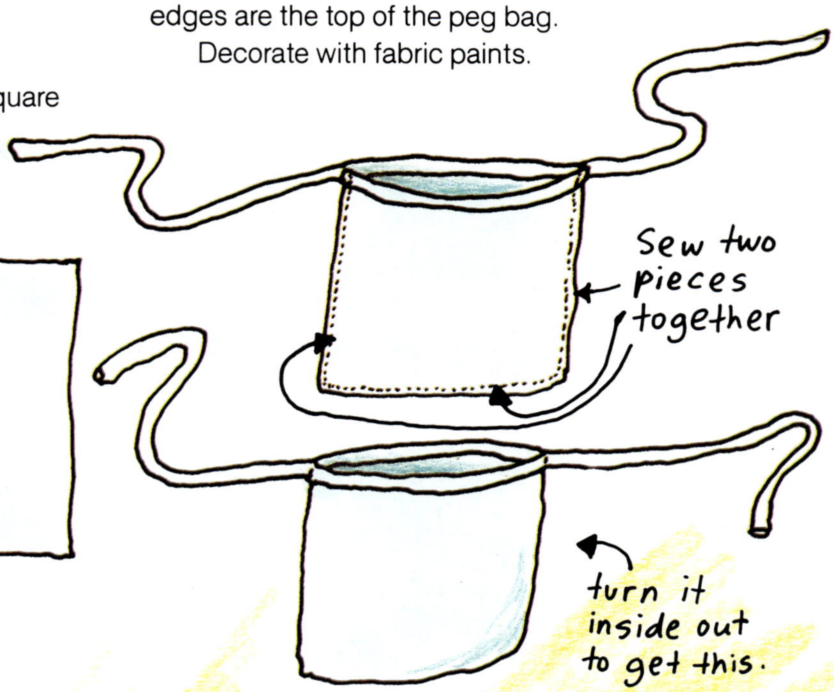

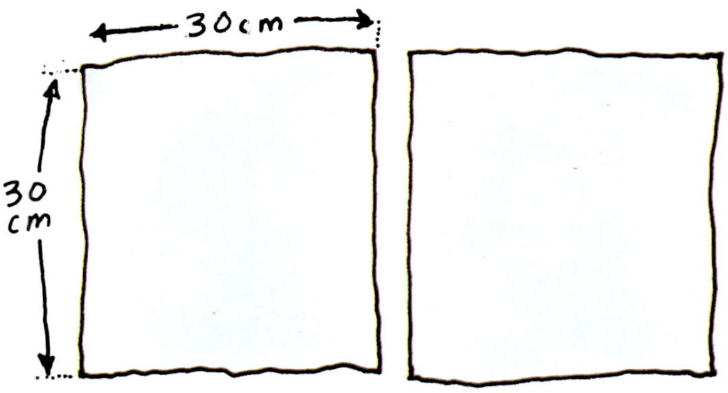

How to make:

Bind one edge of one piece of material with bias binding. Take the second piece of material and pin the centre of the remaining bias binding in the centre of the material. Bind the material, leaving the ends of the bias binding to be the ties for the peg bag (as shown).

Biscuits and pickles

Both are simple to make. They will look even more attractive if, before filling the bottles, you decorate the screw-top jars with fancy designs which you can paint on with poster paints.

Old favourites

You will need:
½ cup margarine
2 cups sugar
4 cups self-raising flour
pinch of salt
vanilla
2 eggs
peanuts
sultanas

How to make:
Melt the margarine and allow to cool. Beat the eggs. Pour the melted margarine into a bowl and add the sugar, flour, pinch of salt and beaten eggs. Then add a few drops of vanilla. Mix together thoroughly. Place the mixture in the fridge to chill before rolling.

When chilled, divide the mixture in half. Add the peanuts to one half and the sultanas to the other. Roll each mixture into a long sausage shape, then cut into small pieces, placing on tray ready to bake in a moderate oven for about 15 minutes.

Allow to cool before packing into air tight jars.

Bread and butter cucumbers

You will need:

small green cucumbers – enough to fill a 2 litre jug
4 large white onions – sliced down not round
2 ½ cups sugar
2 ½ cups cider vinegar
¾ teaspoon turmeric
½ teaspoon celery seed
1 tablespoon mustard seeds
¼ cup salt
1 litre crushed ice

How to make:

Thinly slice the cucumbers into a 2 litre jug, tip into a large bowl. Add the sliced onions, then sprinkle with salt and cover with ice. Leave this to stand for three hours.

Drain off and then rinse the whole mixture thoroughly with cold water. Place in saucepan and add the remaining ingredients. Slowly bring this mixture almost to the boil, but do not let it boil. Stir frequently.

Allow to cool, then carefully ladle into screw-top jars.

Paint and paper

Make a poster
This gives you the opportunity to make a very personal gift for someone special. Choose something you know they are interested in or love to do. This means you could make a pop star poster (for the young at heart), a tide chart poster (for the boating enthusiast), or a book poster (for the bookworm), anything – you just have to find interesting pieces in magazines and cut them out.

You will need:
1 sheet of thick cardboard
lots of magazines
glue
felt-tip pens

How to make:
Say it's a pop star poster you have decided to make. Go through all the old magazines, TV magazines and newspapers, cutting out photographs of the stars, bits of information about them or their record sales. It may take several months to collect enough material but cut it out as you find it and keep it flat in a folder until you are ready to start.

When ready, spread out all the material you have collected and trim it neatly.

On a sheet of scrap paper roughly plan out your design before gluing the pieces onto the cardboard and adding borders, designs, comments and colour with the felt-tip pens. Use coloured cardboard if it makes the photographs look better.

Window fun

A great idea to brighten up a window. The more light that can come through, the better the effect.

You will need:

1 sheet of thin black cardboard
cellophane paper – various colours
sticky tape
scissors

How to make:

Plan your design first on a sheet of scrap paper, this way you will solve all the problems without wasting any of your precious materials. Remember, simple shapes are the most effective, and place all large shapes in the middle of your cardboard (the edges need the strength and it prevents tearing).

Having decided on your pattern or picture, outline the shapes, in pencil, on the cardboard and cut out. If you make a hole with the point of the scissors first, it makes cutting easier and less likely to tear.

When all the cutting out is finished, carefully cut the cellophane to fit on the back of the cardboard. Use the sticky tape to attach.

Windy presents

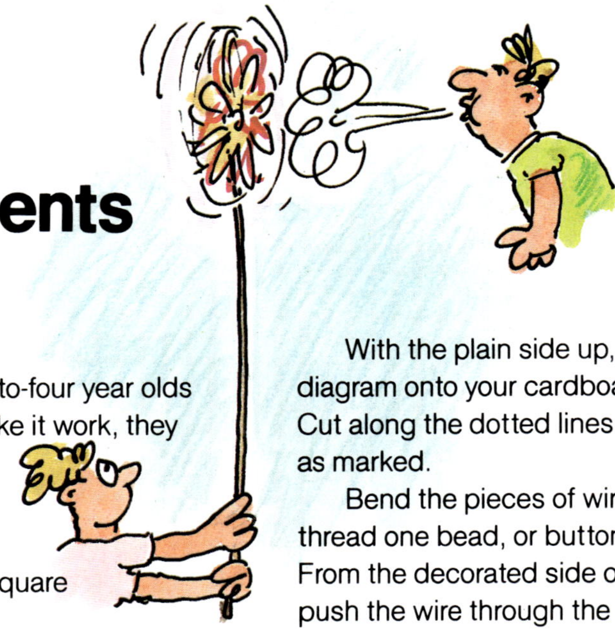

A helter-skelter windmill

The ideal present for the two-to-four year olds in your family because, to make it work, they have to turn around madly.

You will need:

various coloured paints
1 piece of cardboard 26 cm square
2 beads or round buttons
1 piece of stiff wire 20 cm long (a coat-hanger will do)
1 piece of dowel 50 cm long
binding tape

How to make:

First paint a design of stripes or spots on one side of the cardboard. When it is dry, paint the other side a plain colour.

With the plain side up, carefully draw the diagram onto your cardboard, then cut out. Cut along the dotted lines and make five holes as marked.

Bend the pieces of wire (as shown), then thread one bead, or button, onto the wire. From the decorated side of the cardboard push the wire through the centre hole, then carefully bend each of the remaining four holes onto the wire. Fit the second bead on and bend the wire over to stop it coming off (the distance between the two beads should be about 5 cm).

Now bind the wire tightly onto the dowel with tape.

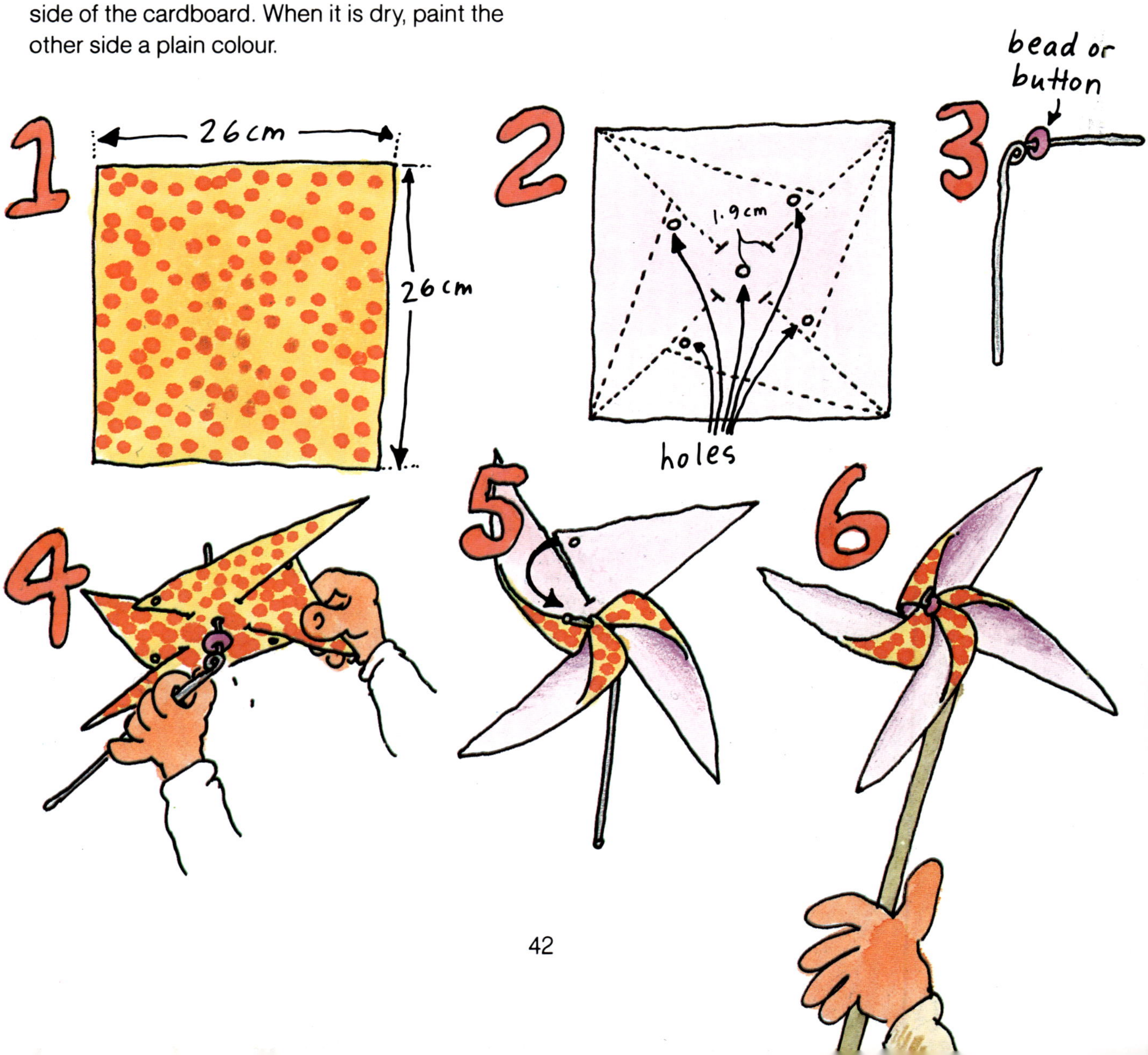

Wind chimes

Wind chimes add a pleasant sound to the garden, so make a set for your gardening friends.

You will need:

2 small plastic garden pots, one smaller than the other
various coloured paints
hand drill and bit
30-40 milk bottle tops
darning needle and cotton
1 piece of thick string
2 small sticks (matches are ideal)

How to make:

First clean the garden pots thoroughly, then paint some great patterns all over the outsides. When the paint is thoroughly dry, use a hand drill and a small bit to make a series of tiny holes around the rim of the pots.

Round out the milk bottle tops into a nice shape, then, using the darning needle and cotton, attach them to the rim of each pot so that they hang down about 15 cm. Tie firmly with a reef knot.

Thread the string up through the drainage hole of each pot, knotting the string to a matchstick across the hole. Keep both pots about 10 cm apart. Extend the string at least 30 cm above the top of the wind chime so that it can be hung in the garden, or in a window.

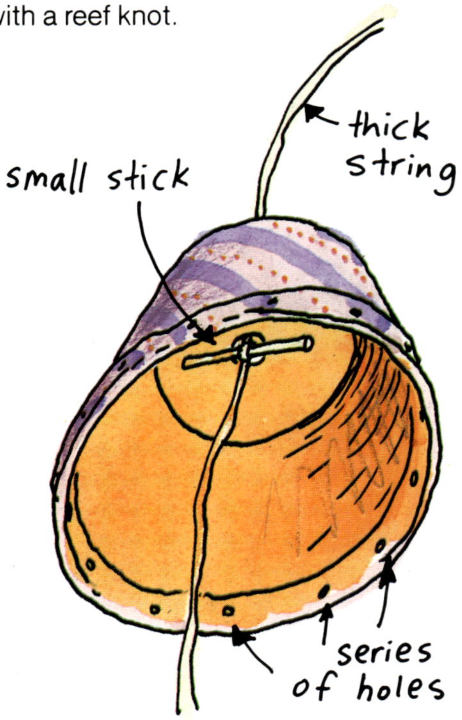

Odds and ends

Garden signs

Gardening friends and relatives will love this present – it will help them remember what they have planted where!

You will need:

square plastic ice cream containers with lids
selection of coloured marking pens
scissors

How to make:

Measure and cut pieces from the flat sides, the bottom and the lid of the ice cream containers. These pieces should be 5 cm wide and 15 cm long, with one end shaped to a point (as shown).

Decide what seeds are likely to be planted, such as: lettuce, tomato, radish, petunia, pansy, or even weeds!

With a black marking pen, print the names *down* the plastic (as shown). Do not go below where the sign will be in the ground. With the coloured marking pens, decorate each sign appropriately.

Pack about 10 different signs together to make a great gift.

Hand puppets

A set of hand puppets make a fun gift for the whole family.

You will need:

small plastic bottles or balloons
newspaper
glue
poster paints
scraps of wool
old scarf
elastic bands

How to make:

Small plastic drink bottles, or small inflated balloons, make an ideal base on which to construct the puppet's head. Tear up lots of newspaper, cover the bottle or balloon with glue and stick on the pieces of newspaper. Keep adding layers, building the shape of the head as you go. Don't forget extra for the nose, which can be any shape you want!

When the glue is thoroughly dry, paint the head. Wait for the paint to dry before adding in eyes, mouth and ears. Cut the wool into lengths and glue on as hair.

The scarf is used to cover your hand and then use your thumb and two fingers as arms for the puppet. To keep the scarf in place, fit rubber bands (as shown).

Use your two centre fingers to operate the head. Design a whole family of puppets, then write your own play for them to perform.

Wrap it up

Having made the presents, why not make your own wrapping paper, cards and fancy boxes?

You will need:
several sheets of white cardboard
felt-tip pens – various colours
poster paints – various colours
tissue paper – various colours
cardboard boxes – various shapes
margarine cartons, with their lids
sheets of white paper (try lining paper)
paper glue
contact glue
several potatoes
several old saucers

Cards

How to make:
Take a sheet of white cardboard and cut it into pieces 30 cm x 10 cm, then score along the dotted lines (as shown). Fold the cardboard into a zigzag shape. This is the basic card and now it's over to you to let your imagination run riot and create cards to suit the people or the occasion.

You can make a collage card, using the various coloured tissue papers, gluing them onto the card in a mad design, or a planned picture (such as a garden of flowers).

You can use the felt-tip pens to create a personalised card, doing a portrait of your friend with their name on the front.

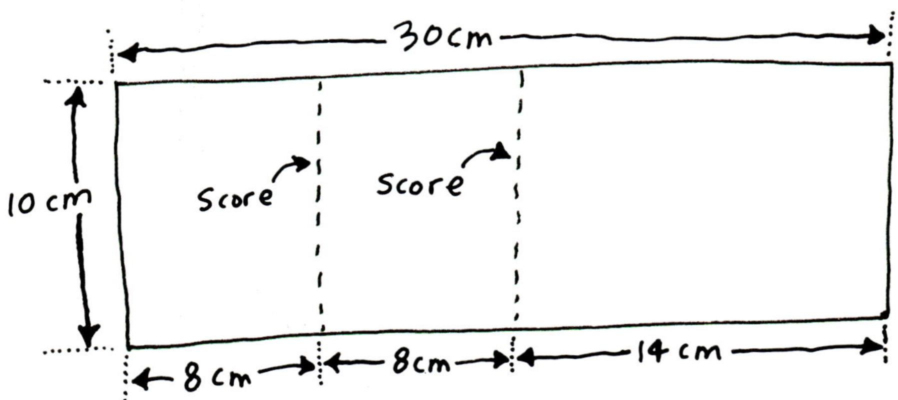

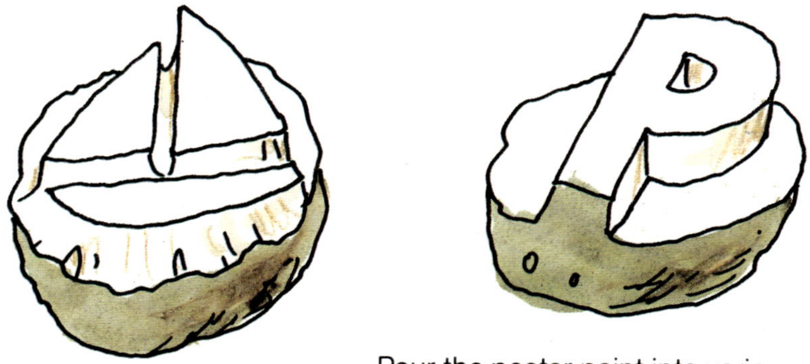

Paper

How to make:

The sheets of white lining paper can turn into great wrapping paper if you decorate them with potato prints.

Cut your potatoes in half, then carefully make the designs by cutting away the parts of the potato not required. You can create shapes such as stars and triangles, or squares and circles, then you make up your own patterns on the paper using poster paint.

Pour the poster paint into various saucers, one for each colour, dip the potato cut into the paint then press it on the paper. A word of warning: *don't fill the saucers too full, you will end up with paint all over the place and it's easy enough to add more as needed.*

Leave the paper flat to dry; however, if you want to create a streaky effect, hang it over the clothes line while the paint is still wet.

Fancy boxes

How to make:

For the gift that needs its own fancy container, here's an idea or two.

Take a cardboard box – find one that's the right size for the gift – then decorate the outside, *and* the inside, using the poster paints. You can put the paint on with a brush, then add your design when this has dried, using a brush or the potato cuts.

To make the lid fancy, paste cut-up strips of tissue paper on the top, using paper glue. The other alternative is to do a collage using paper, or shells or buttons. Remember to paint in a background colour first.